South San Francisco Public Library

3 9048 08755551 6

W9-CEI-335

S.S.F. Public Library
West Orange
840 West Orange Ave.
South San Francisco, CA 94080

NOV   2010

DEMCO

NIC BISHOP
LIZARDS

scholastic 💡 nonfiction
an imprint of
📖 SCHOLASTIC

The author wishes to thank the John Ball Zoo as well as
Tony and Kari Collison for their help with this book.

Copyright © 2010 by Nic Bishop.
Page 3 photography by Nic Bishop,
copyright © 1999 Wright Group Publishing, Inc.
All rights reserved. Published by Scholastic Inc.
SCHOLASTIC, SCHOLASTIC NONFICTION, and associated logos
are trademarks and/or registered trademarks of Scholastic Inc.

No part of this publication may be reproduced, stored in a retrieval system,
or transmitted in any form or by any means, electronic, mechanical,
photocopying, recording, or otherwise, without written permission of the
publisher. For information regarding permission, write to Scholastic Inc.,
Attention: Permissions Department, 557 Broadway, New York, NY 10012.

LIBRARY OF CONGRESS CATALOGING-IN-PUBLICATION DATA
Bishop, Nic, 1955– • Nic Bishop lizards. • p. cm.
1. Lizards—Juvenile literature. I. Title. II.
Title: Lizards.
QL666.L2B57 2010 • 597.95—dc22 • 2009046450

ISBN 978-0-545-20634-1
10 9 8 7 6 5 4 3 2 1   10 11 12 13 14

Printed in Singapore 46
First printing, October 2010
Book design by Nancy Sabato

The magnification of animals shown at actual size
or larger is indicated in parentheses.

This gliding gecko from Southeast Asia
has webbed feet and flaps of skin on its
body, which it uses like a parachute to
glide from branch to branch.

The lizard on the title page is an
Australian bearded dragon.
(shown at 2 times actual size)

LIZARDS
lead lives that
are full of surprises.

They live in the tallest of trees and the hottest of deserts.
They glide through the air, swim through the water, and
scamper upside down across ceilings. Some run on four
legs, some run on two, and some wriggle on their bellies,
on no legs at all.

*Lizards were around more than 150 million years ago, at the
time of the dinosaurs, and some probably stole dinosaur eggs
for food. But this small crocodile skink from New Guinea
prefers to hunt insects and worms.*
(shown at 4 times actual size)

Some lizards do not have legs. Glass lizards slither like snakes through meadows and forests. But a close look reveals that they are not snakes. Glass lizards can blink, and they have ear holes. Snakes do not have eyelids, or ears that you can see.

(shown at 3 times actual size)

There are about 5,000 types of lizards.

They include iguanas, chameleons, geckos, skinks, and monitors, and they come in more shapes and sizes than you might imagine. The largest lizard, the Komodo dragon from Indonesia, is big enough to kill a water buffalo. The smallest, a dwarf gecko from the Caribbean, is so tiny that it can get caught in spiderwebs. It is small enough to curl up on your thumbnail, yet it has the same skeleton, muscles, stomach, and beating heart as other lizards. In fact, it has most of the same organs as you.

Lizards are reptiles, like snakes, turtles, and crocodiles. And like other reptiles, they lay eggs that are protected by a shell, so they can be laid on land. These bearded dragon eggs are hatching about two months after they were laid.

(shown at 6 times actual size)

Lizards hatch from eggs, which might be hidden underground, beneath a log, or even in a termite nest. A mother lizard is careful to find a moist and safe place for her eggs. Lizard eggs often have thin shells and dry out if left in the open. They are also a favorite snack for many animals, including other lizards.

There are some lizards that do not lay their eggs. Instead, the mother holds them inside her body, to keep them safe and warm until they hatch. Then she gives birth to wriggling babies. A few skinks, such as shingleback skinks from Australia, even nourish the growing babies they carry inside, much like mammals do. Shingleback babies are born almost half as long as their mothers.

9

Whether it is born as a wriggling baby or hatches from an egg, a young lizard is left to look after itself. Luckily it comes equipped to do just that. Each little lizard looks like a miniature version of its parents. It has legs for running, claws for gripping, and a tail for balance. It scampers away as soon as it is ready.

At first, a baby lizard can only rely on the knowledge it was born with, called *instinct*, to hunt for food and hide from predators. Unlike a mammal, a lizard does not have parents who protect it and teach it what to do. This can make growing up tough. A little lizard has enemies to watch out for and lessons to learn. But if it stays safe, a lizard may live for five, ten, or even twenty years. Once, a lizard called a slow worm lived in a zoo until it was fifty-four years old.

Soon after hatching, a baby veiled chameleon will climb into the trees to search for its first insect meal. On pages 36–37 you can see how this lizard looks when it grows up.
(shown at 5 times actual size)

A baby lizard has a coat of special skin, just like its parents. This skin is covered with scales, and each scale is made of *keratin*, the same bendy stuff your fingernails are made of. It is wonderfully waterproof, which means that lizards can live in hot, sunny places without drying out. **What's more, lizard skin comes in a wardrobe of snazzy styles.** It can be as hard as armor or as soft as velvet. Iguana skin has spines like a storybook dragon's. And there are colors, too, from red to blue. Chameleons even change colors to tell one another what mood they are in.

In time, a young lizard will outgrow its skin. Besides, even the shiniest suit of armor will get scratched and scuffed. So a lizard usually *molts* several times each year. The old skin peels off in pieces to reveal a bright new one underneath.

A shingleback skink's skin has large bony plates for protection. Some people call this lizard the two-headed skink. Its plump tail confuses predators.

(shown at actual size)

Lizards are often called cold-blooded *because their body temperature depends on the environment. Marine iguanas from the Galápagos Islands get very chilled when they dive under the sea to eat seaweed. So they lie in the sun afterward, until their bodies are about as warm as yours.*

Most lizards live in warm parts of the world because their body temperature depends on their surroundings. Each morning a lizard finds a sunny spot, perhaps on a rock or a branch, to stretch out and soak up the heat. It needs to warm its body quickly. Otherwise it will be too cold and sluggish to hunt for food or run from predators.

Mammals like dogs, horses, and humans keep warm in a different way. We mammals use energy from the food we eat, which is why we are always hungry. **By using the sun's energy for warmth, lizards get by on little food.** The amount of food a mammal needs in one day can last a lizard for two weeks. That is why lizards survive so well in places where there is not much to eat, like deserts.

Deserts are great places to find lizards.

After all, there is plenty of sun to keep them warm.

Of course, sometimes it can get too warm, even for a lizard. So most do their errands early in the morning. You will spot them scuttling across the sand before the sun gets too high. Once it's hot, they duck under a shady rock or dive into a cool burrow.

Other desert lizards avoid the heat by living under the sand. These types of lizards are called sand swimmers. Many have snakelike bodies with tiny legs, or no legs at all. They slither beneath the surface like fish, hunting for termites, grubs, and other insects.

The shield-tailed agama from Africa is small, so it has to watch out for many predators. At night, it blocks its burrow with its round, spiny tail so it can sleep safely.
(shown at 4 times actual size)

Lizards often have clever ways of walking in the desert. Web-footed geckos from Africa have feet like snowshoes to clamber across powdery sand. Shovel-snouted lizards, also from Africa, hop from one foot to the other, trying to keep them off the hot surface. Desert lizards often also have see-through scales that cover their eyes like goggles to keep out the sand. If their goggles get scratched, that's no problem. The lizard replaces them along with the rest of its skin when it molts.

If you explore the desert at night, you will find a whole new crew of lizards running around. These nocturnal lizards are geckos. They come out of their burrows at sunset to chase insects, spiders, and scorpions.

Knob-tailed geckos hunt in the Australian Outback after sunset, when it is cooler. Their large, sensitive eyes help them chase down insects by moonlight.
(shown at 4 times actual size)

The thorny devil from Australia has an amazing way to get drinking water. It rubs its belly on damp sand, and tiny channels in its skin pull water from the ground to its mouth. A thorny devil eats only ants. It laps them up with a sticky tongue, one by one.
(shown at 3 times actual size)

Insects, spiders, and scorpions don't sound like fun to eat. But their juicy bodies provide water as well as food. In fact, some desert lizards almost never drink. They get most of their water from what they eat instead. Other lizards lap dew from plants early in the morning. The web-footed gecko even licks dew from its own back.

But sometimes living conditions just get too tough. Then, a lizard may head deep into its burrow. Its breathing and heart rate slow as it enters a very deep sleep. This lets it survive for weeks or even months, until rain falls and things get better. The Gila monster from North America is the ultimate desert survivor. It is thought to be able to stay underground for several years.

Life in a forest is very different from life in a desert. Lizards that live here are expert climbers. Chameleons, for instance, have special feet. Each looks like a mitten with two fingers that clamp tight to branches. Chameleons also have *prehensile tails* to curl around things for extra grip.

The most amazing feet, however, belong to geckos. Their toe pads are often covered in hairs that are so tiny you need a powerful microscope to see them. Molecules on each hair cling like little magnets to molecules on the leaf or branch the gecko is walking on. A single molecule does not cling well on its own. But there are billions of molecules on a hair and millions of hairs on a gecko's toes. Together, they grip so well that many geckos can climb glass and walk upside down across ceilings without ever slipping.

Jackson's chameleons live in Africa. Males use their large horns to wrestle with one another. Chameleons can't hear very well because they have no ear holes. But they can feel vibrations through their bodies instead.
(shown at 3 times actual size)

Getting from one tree to the next can be tricky. Chameleons are nervous crossing the forest floor. They move one foot at a time, looking this way and that for predators. **The flying dragon from Southeast Asia has a safer way to travel between trees.** It can glide for a hundred feet and steer through the air to land just where it wants. Few predators can match that.

Staying safe is important to a lizard, especially when it is asleep. Many cling to the ends of thin branches. That way, if a snake creeps up, the branch will tremble and wake the lizard so it can leap to safety. If the branch hangs over water, the lizard just dives in. It will hold its legs flat to its sides and swim away like a fish. Some lizards can stay underwater for an hour.

This leaf-tailed gecko from Madagascar lives in the forest undergrowth. It clings to a twig when it sleeps and carefully twists its body to look just like a wrinkly old leaf.
(shown at 4 times actual size)

Flying dragons open flaps of skin like wings to glide from tree to tree. They are so good at it that they only come to the ground to lay their eggs.

(shown at 2 times actual size)

Of course, if hiding doesn't work, there is always plan B. Run! A frightened lizard will usually sprint straight for its favorite hideout. The basilisk lizard does one better. It runs straight across water to escape predators. Extra-large feet with flaps of skin on each toe help stop it from breaking through the water's surface. But its main trick is to run really fast. **A basilisk sprints at up to twenty steps a second, so its feet barely have time to sink.** Scientists have calculated that a human would have to run sixty-five miles an hour to cross water like a basilisk does.

Basilisks, which grow to about two feet long, live close to water in the rain forests of South and Central America, so they are always ready to make a quick getaway.

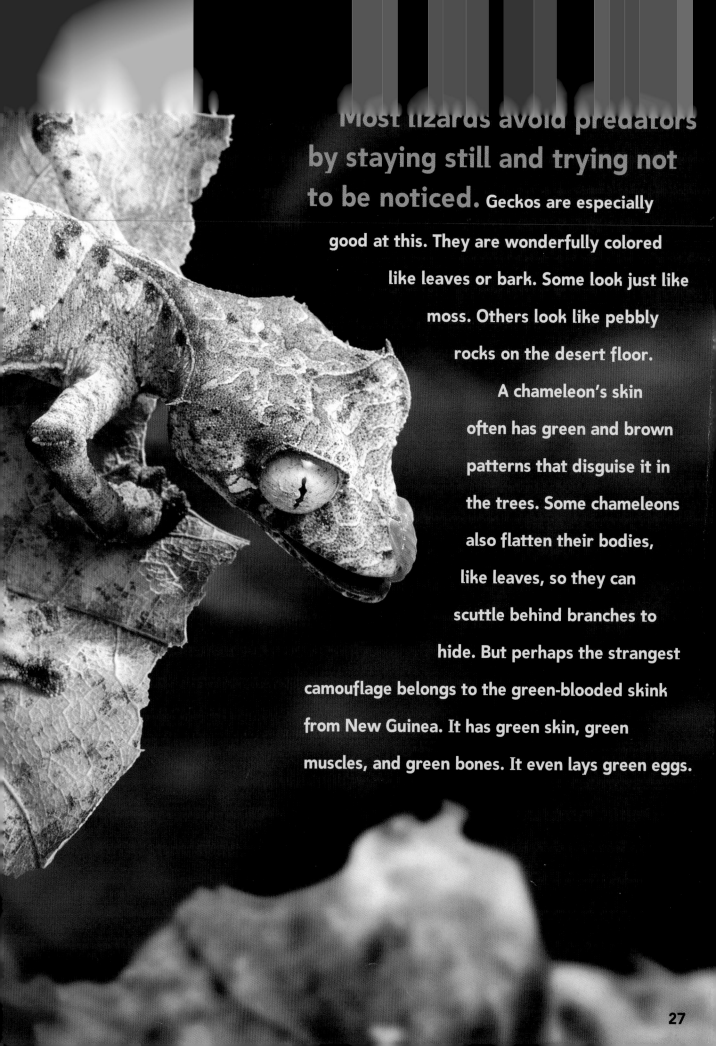

Most lizards avoid predators by staying still and trying not to be noticed. Geckos are especially good at this. They are wonderfully colored like leaves or bark. Some look just like moss. Others look like pebbly rocks on the desert floor. A chameleon's skin often has green and brown patterns that disguise it in the trees. Some chameleons also flatten their bodies, like leaves, so they can scuttle behind branches to hide. But perhaps the strangest camouflage belongs to the green-blooded skink from New Guinea. It has green skin, green muscles, and green bones. It even lays green eggs.

Other lizards try to scare predators away. Shingleback skinks poke out bright blue tongues and hiss. Thorny devils swallow air and inflate their bodies like puffer fish. They look too big and prickly to swallow. Chuckwallas from North America dive into rocky cracks and then inflate their bodies. They become so wedged in that nothing can pull them out. The weirdest lizards in North America, though, are horned lizards. Some squirt bad-tasting blood from their eyes to foil coyotes.

The Australian frilled dragon has a large ruffle of skin around its head which pops open like an umbrella to scare predators. Even a baby like this one has a ruffle.

(shown at 2 times actual size)

Even if a predator grabs it by the tail, a lizard still has a way to escape. The tail falls off! Many lizards have tails that break off easily, with little bleeding. The broken piece jiggles and twitches like an excited worm to keep the predator busy while its owner slips away. The lizard will usually grow a new tail. And some skinks do not even waste the old one. They go back to find it. Then they eat it!

Some geckos even wriggle out of their skins to slip away from predators! Lizards seem to know every escape trick in the book. But this is no surprise. They are on the menu for almost every animal out there. Even other lizards eat them.

Some lizards have bright blue tails to tempt a predator to grab that part first. Then the tail breaks off so the lizard can escape.
(shown at 3 times actual size)

Only a few lizards, such as iguanas and chuckwallas, eat plants. Most are predators, and they can be sneaky. A chameleon stays still as it waits for its prey to come close. Its eyes do all the moving. They twist and turn, and even look two ways at once to search for food. A cricket will do nicely.

Then the chameleon checks out its target. Its special eyes magnify things. And they can tell how far away the prey is just by focusing on it. That is important because next the chameleon will open its mouth, and splat! It spits its sticky tongue out just the right distance to grab its dinner.

Geckos stalk their prey at night, like cats do. They creep close, then pounce. Moths and mosquitoes barely have a chance.

In the blink of an eye, this veiled chameleon's tongue has stretched almost twelve inches long. The chameleon is using its prehensile tail to help it reach for its meal. It has turned beautiful colors with excitement, too.

The sneakiest hunter of all is the sandfish.

It swims beneath the deserts of northern Africa and western Asia by wriggling its body through the sand like a little shark. Super senses allow it to detect the vibrations of spiders and insects on the surface above. Then it strikes from below.

There are other strange lizardlike creatures called blind lizards and worm lizards that almost never come to the surface. Most have no legs, since legs only get in the way when wriggling underground. They can also barely see, since eyes have little use in the darkness. They probably find their prey by taste or by feeling vibrations. But nobody knows very much about their lives. Most of these animals have never been studied properly.

The sandfish is a sand swimmer. It has a streamlined body and super-smooth skin to slip through sand dunes. Its skin is incredibly scratch resistant. It can survive sandblasting better than steel.

(shown at 3 times actual size)

A monitor tracks down prey like a supersleuth. It has a forked tongue, which it flicks into the air to pick up chemical clues. Then it wipes its tongue across a special organ in its mouth. This organ tastes the tiniest amounts of chemical scent. And if it tastes prey, the monitor will hunt. It checks every cranny with its tongue. Many monitors will climb trees, swim rivers, and dig out burrows to find prey. Some monitors can even outrun people. And they have been known to swallow animals almost as long as themselves. A well-fed monitor will wander along with its victim's tail sticking out of its mouth until its stomach has made room for the rest.

Monitors are the most clever lizards. Two African Nile monitors often help each other to raid crocodile nests. One distracts the mother crocodile while the other snatches her eggs. An adult Nile monitor grows six feet long. This one is a baby.
(shown at 2 times actual size)

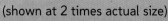

A Komodo dragon may compare
the chemical clues on each fork
of its tongue to figure which way
its prey has gone. It eats pigs,
goats, lizards, and even vipers and
cobras. But its favorite meal is a
dead deer or buffalo.

The Komodo dragon is the king of all monitors. It can grow ten feet long, with teeth almost an inch in size. These teeth have cutting edges like saw blades, and they are always sharp. The Komodo replaces them as they wear out by growing as many as 200 new teeth each year.

A Komodo dragon's favorite hunting plan is to wait near an animal trail for a pig or a deer to come by. One big bite will weaken its prey because the Komodo is one of a few lizards to have *venom*. **The Komodo dragon is the world's largest venomous animal.** Even if a victim escapes, it often dies of its wounds. And a hungry Komodo can sense a dead animal from over two miles away.

A monitor lizard also uses its tongue to find a mate. The male follows perfumes, called *pheromones*, which the female produces. When they meet, the monitors gently lick each other and nuzzle. It's their way of talking.

For other lizards, courtship is a chance to dance and show off.

Iguanas and chameleons bob their heads and strut back and forth. Anole lizards open flaps of colored skin under their chins, like little flags. Most geckos come out at night when it is too dark for a mate to see them dance. So they sing instead. They chirp and yap like excited frogs.

After mating, a female finds a place for her eggs. Some lizards lay one or two eggs at a time. Others lay dozens. They might be as big as apples or as tiny as freckles. But big or small, each egg contains a new life. And it is just waiting to wriggle into the world.

Chameleons change color when they are excited, sleepy, or cold, or when they want to show off. This colorful male panther chameleon is showing off to a mate. Normally he is dark green all over.
(shown at 2 times actual size)

Trying to find an animal in the wild can become an adventure filled with uncertainty and surprise. This was particularly true for the thorny devil on pages 20–21.

The thorny devil is one of the most amazing-looking lizards in the world, so naturally it was at the top of my list to photograph for this book. The only problem was finding one. They are rare, hard to spot, and live only in the remote deserts of Australia.

First, I phoned a ranger at an isolated station in Australia to get some clues. "Just drive along the Shark Bay Road," he said quite simply. "You see them all the time."

Feeling excited, I packed my bags, flew to Perth in Western Australia, and drove north into the searing heat for two days. Eventually, I came to the spot the ranger had suggested, and I looked. And looked. There were no thorny devils! So I tracked down the ranger and asked him another question, which I realize I should have asked before I began my trip: "When, exactly, did you last see a thorny devil?" He looked at me, paused thoughtfully, and admitted that he hadn't seen one in four years!

Well, I was in far too deep to give up now. I just drove, day after day, creeping along remote desert roads at twenty miles an hour, gazing at the sand for thorny devils. I stopped at every prickly-looking bit of wood. A family of emus wandered by, surprised to see me miles from anywhere. Then, after hundreds of miles, I rounded a corner and there it was: a thorny devil, right in front of me. I had to pinch myself to make sure I was not dreaming.

Many other lizards were photographed in captivity, in my studio. But that does not mean it was easy. I stayed up all night waiting for the bearded dragons on page 8 to hatch. I spent weeks getting the veiled chameleon on pages 36–37 to stretch as far as it possibly could to catch a cricket (and if I moved that cricket half an inch farther to the right than in the photograph, the chameleon would just stand on its branch and give me a very cross look). But the trickiest project was photographing the basilisk lizard running on water.

Because I used a lot of electronic gear for this photograph, I could not take it in a real rain forest pool. So I built a pool in my garage and heated it with large aquarium heaters. It took weeks to set up the lights, the laser triggers, and other things I needed. Then I was ready to photograph some basilisks, which I got from a person who bred them. But no matter what I did, they never ran across the surface. They dived in and swam to the bottom to hide. I tried building takeoff ramps. I tried swapping lizards. I tried trick after trick. Nothing worked!

Eventually, I wondered if it was taking me too long to carry a basilisk from its cage in my house to the pond in the garage. Perhaps if I moved the rain forest pond inside my house, that would work? It seemed like a crazy idea, but luckily my wife understood. More weeks followed as I rebuilt the pond indoors. Then the moment arrived. I plucked a basilisk from its cage, and to my delight, it buzzed across the water surface like a speedboat. Now, after almost two months, I was ready to start taking photographs!

Index Entries in **bold** indicate photographs.

Further Reading

Davies, Valerie, and Chris Mattison. *World of Animals*. Vols. 44–46. New York: Grolier. 2003–2005.

Facklam, Margery. *Lizards: Weird and Wonderful*. New York: Little, Brown. 2003.

McCarthy, Colin. *Eyewitness: Reptile*. London: DK Children. 2000.

    To learn about how Nic created this book, and the books he researched before writing the text, visit www.nicbishop.com.

Glossary

Molt To periodically shed an outer layer, such as skin, shell, hair, feathers, or horns.

Predator An animal that lives by hunting other animals for food.

Prehensile tail A tail that can seize or grasp something by wrapping around it.

Prey An animal that is hunted by another animal for food.

Venom A poison that passes into a victim's body through a bite or sting.